W9-AYH-409

OUR PLANET

Deserts

RICHARD STEPHEN

Troll Associates

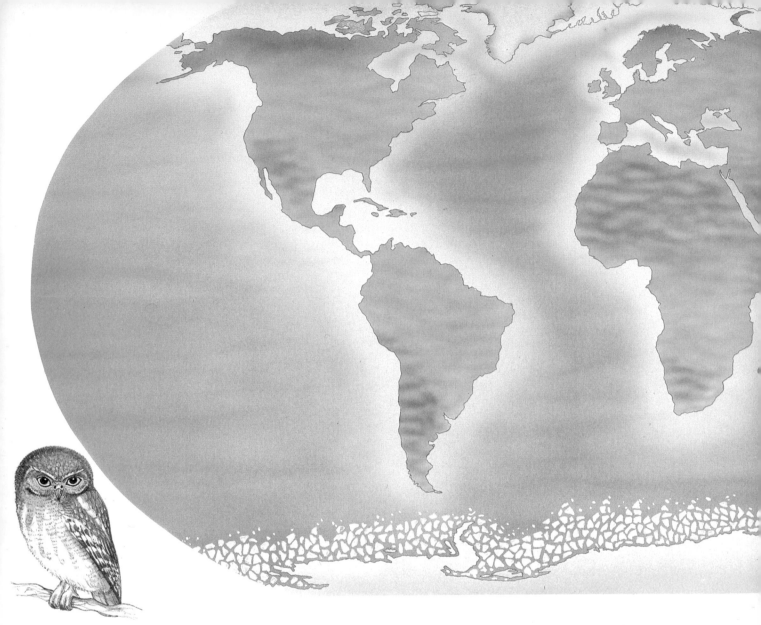

Published by Troll Associates, Mahwah, New Jersey 07430

Copyright © 1990 by Eagle Books Limited

All rights reserved. No part of this book may be reproduced or utilized in any form or by any means, electronic or mechanical, including photocopying, recording or by any storage and retrieval system, without permission in writing from the Publisher.

Design by James Marks, London.

Picture research by Jan Croot.

Illustrators: Dee McLean: pages 12-13; Sebastian Quigley: pages 6-7, 18; Paul Sullivan: page 10; Ian Thompson: pages 2-3; Phil Weare: pages 8, 21, 22, 23, 24, 25, 26-27; Linda Worrall: page 14.

Printed in the U.S.A.

10 9 8 7 6 5 4 3 2 1

Library of Congress Cataloging-in-Publication Data

Stephen, Richard.
    Deserts / by Richard Stephen; illustrated by Dee McLean . . . [et al.].
        p.   cm.—(Our planet)
    Summary: Discusses the characteristics and formation of the world's deserts and how plants, animals, and people have learned to survive there.
    ISBN 0-8167-1969-1 (lib. bdg.)   ISBN 0-8167-1970-5 (pbk.)
    1. Deserts—Juvenile literature.   [1. Deserts.]   I. McLean, Dee, ill. II. Title.   III. Series.
GB612.S74   1990
508.315'4—dc20   89-20300

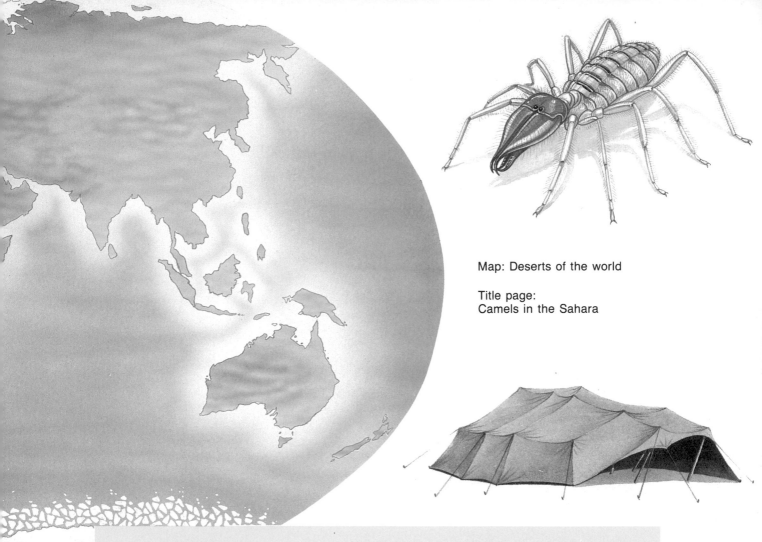

Map: Deserts of the world

Title page:
Camels in the Sahara

CONTENTS

Lands of Rock, Stone, and Sand

Almost everyone's idea of a desert is of endless stretches of sand where travelers lose their way and die of thirst under the burning sun. Such places exist, but there are other kinds of desert, too.

A desert is a place where little or no rain falls. Scientists define a desert as a land with less than 10 inches of rainfall a year. The climate is either too hot or too cold for much plant or animal life. Most deserts are stony or rocky, but there are also salt deserts, where the lack of fresh water restricts life.

The daytime heat of a desert can make the rain evaporate before it reaches the ground. But even the hottest deserts can be very cold at night, when the heat escapes quickly into the cloudless sky.

Many deserts are separated from the sea by mountain ranges. The moisture from the sea falls as rain over the mountains before it can reach the desert beyond. Frozen deserts are found in polar regions. The icy landmass cools the ocean current, causing the winds to lose their moisture over the water before they reach land.

Despite the harsh conditions, some people, plants, and animals live in deserts and have learned ways to survive there.

→ Rounded *dunes*, or sand hills, in the Arabian Desert. Sand blown by the wind piles up into dunes and ridges. In places, rows of dunes stretch as far as the eye can see.

↑ Monument Valley, Arizona. Towers and spires of rock, created by erosion, stand out boldly above the empty landscape. They serve as welcome landmarks for travelers crossing the desert.

→ Crescent-shaped sand dunes called *barchans* are created by wind blowing regularly in one direction. Sand blown along just above the ground carves desert rocks into strange shapes.

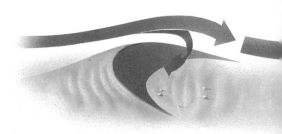

Many features of the desert are the result of *erosion* — the gradual wearing away of rock and stone — over thousands of years. Erosion is caused by wind and water. Parts of the desert landscape were formed by rivers that have long since dried up. As they cut through the soft rock, they carved out dramatic steep-sided valleys, or *canyons*. In places there are also spectacular *plateaus*, or high, flat tables of land. Here the wind and rain have worn away soft rock, leaving "islands" of harder rock towering over the empty landscape.

The continual heating by day and cooling by night help to break the rock into even smaller fragments: first into stones and gravel, finally into grains of sand. Sand blown by the wind is one of the chief causes of erosion in deserts. It is blown into wavelike mounds, or *dunes.* We talk of "shifting" sands because a desert is always on the move.

For years people have struggled to stop the desert from devouring more land. As it advances, it can bring famine and death. New methods are being found to drill deep wells in the search for water. Controlled watering of the land, or *irrigation*, is used to help crops grow. But farmers' misuse of land along the edges of desert, by over-grazing their cattle, for example, is another form of erosion that helps deserts to spread. Desert dwellers are often fighting just to survive, so it is difficult for them to concern themselves with plans for the future.

The Great Sahara

The Sahara is the world's largest desert. Stretching across the top third of Africa, it covers an area about the size of the United States. It spreads over the continent from the Atlantic Ocean to the Red Sea, covering all or part of 11 countries.

The desert is broken only by the rich farmland of the Nile valley and by scattered *oases* – places where there is enough water from wells or springs for dense plant growth. Oases provide good sites for villages or towns. Cairo, the capital of Egypt, was built on an oasis.

The sands for which the Sahara is famous cover only about a tenth of its area. Mountain ranges stretch across the central region, some high enough to have snow on their peaks. Most of the Sahara consists of rocky plateaus and gravelly plains.

Millions of years ago, say scientists, the land occupied by the Sahara was where the South Pole is now.

The one-humped Arabian camels of the Sahara eat even the most prickly plants. Camels can go for long periods without drinking, and most people think they store water in their humps. In fact, the camel's stomach holds a vast amount of water. The fatty hump stores food, and the camel has very little fat elsewhere

← The Arabian camel has one hump and short hair. Because it is so often used as a beast of burden, people sometimes refer to it as "the ship of the desert."

↑ Camels resting near the pyramids at Giza, on the edge of the Sahara Desert. The pyramids are the tombs of the Pharaohs who ruled ancient Egypt. They were built around 2,600 B.C., and are the only one of the Seven Wonders of the World that still exists today.

on its body. After days without eating, the hump looks like a floppy sack.

A camel has long eyelashes to protect its eyes from the sand. It can also close its nostrils to keep sand out of its nose. Its thick knee pads are designed for comfortable kneeling. When a camel walks, its toes spread out and a web of skin between them prevents the foot from sinking into the sand.

Desert Wanderers

To us, deserts are harsh, desolate places. To others, they are home. Many desert dwellers move from one place to another in search of food and water. These people are called *nomads*. The word "nomad" comes from the Greek word for "pasture."

A Mongol of the Gobi Desert.

The land the nomads live on is usually either too hot, too cold, or too dry for permanent farms. So nomads' herds are forced to keep moving to find new grazing land. As the animals move on, the nomads follow, taking their homes with them. The herds provide them with milk, meat, wool, and leather − in fact, almost everything they need to survive.

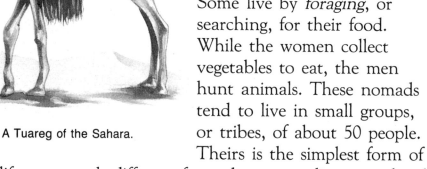

A Tuareg of the Sahara.

Not all nomads are herders. Some live by *foraging*, or searching, for their food. While the women collect vegetables to eat, the men hunt animals. These nomads tend to live in small groups, or tribes, of about 50 people.

Theirs is the simplest form of life, not much different from the way earliest man lived. Nomads are found in the deserts of Africa, Asia, and Australia. Others wander through the jungles and grasslands of Africa. But many are now giving up this way of life and moving to towns.

The San people, or Bushmen, of the Kalahari

A Kalahari Bushman.

↑ A meeting of Bedouins in Jordan. Tents, carpets, cooking utensils and even furniture have to travel everywhere with these nomadic people.

Desert in southern Africa and the Aborigines in Australia wear hardly any clothing. Most other desert wanderers, such as the Tuaregs of the Sahara and the Bedouins of the Middle East, wrap themselves in loose clothing as protection against sun and sand. However, many of those desert wanderers who have abandoned their traditional way of life have taken to wearing clothing more appropriate to their new lifestyle.

11

↑ Nomads in Iran looking for new pasture for their herd of sheep and goats. They are driving the animals from scrub desert up into the hills.

Around the world, nomadic lifestyles are very similar to each other, though customs vary from place to place. Nomads have few belongings other than their weapons and their animals, since possessions make it harder to move.

A Tuareg skin tent.

← In summer the Tuareg people build simple grass tents, but when the weather becomes cooler they use goatskin tents.

The Bedouins of Arabia make their living by rearing camels to sell at markets in oasis towns. They may also tend herds of sheep and goats. They live in tribes, with a chief, or sheikh, as their leader. Recently, many Bedouins have begun to settle in oasis towns.

The Tuaregs of North Africa are Muslims, as are the Bedouins. They worship Allah and follow the teachings of Mohammed. In most Muslim countries the women wear veils. Among the Tuaregs, the men do. This custom may be a practical way of protecting themselves from the desert sand, but even in their camps the veil is seldom removed. Tuaregs were once famous for controlling the caravan trade in slaves, ivory, and gold, but these days they are herders. Their population has been greatly reduced by starvation.

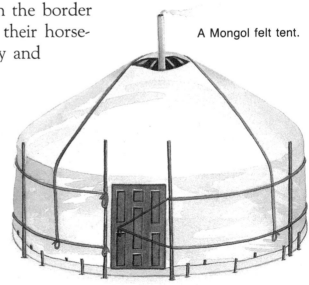

A Bedouin cloth tent.

A Mongol felt tent.

The Mongols live in the Gobi Desert, on the border of China and Russia. They are known for their horse-riding skills and love sports such as archery and wrestling. They wear sheepskin clothing and leather boots to protect themselves against the bitter cold of the open *steppes*, the level, treeless lands where they roam. Many have abandoned their traditional life and have moved to towns or ranches.

Nomads set up camp when they find new grazing land. Their tents can be put up and taken down quickly, and are easy to carry.

The San people were the original inhabitants of most of southern Africa, but now there are few left. As other tribes moved south, they captured the San's hunting grounds. The arrival of European settlers reduced their numbers further. The San are skillful hunters and have an interesting way of collecting water. They suck it up from under the ground with reeds and store it in ostrich eggshells.

The Aborigines are believed to have arrived in Australia by boat from Southeast Asia almost 40,000 years ago. There are hundreds of Aboriginal tribal groups, each occupying a particular part of the country and speaking a different language. They share food and possessions, and each tribe has its own set of rules and rituals.

The most famous Aborigine weapon is the boomerang, a flat, curved throwing stick which returns to the thrower. It is used mainly for sport, while nonreturning ones are used for hunting. Spears are another favorite weapon. The women use sticks to dig for bulbs and roots. As they wander, they make camps of windbreaks and shelters around watering holes, where they believe the spirits of their ancestors live. They understand the land they live in, even knowing when to set fire to it in order to make it more fertile. They believe that all things — people, plants, animals, and even rocks — are important parts of the spirit world.

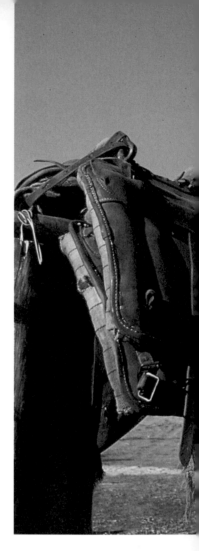

Opposite: Some Aborigines now herd cattle on ranches (top). Others prefer the nomadic way of life (bottom).

→ A San girl drinking water from an ostrich eggshell.

14

15

Water in the Desert

Even the driest deserts may have water underground, called *groundwater*. By digging wells this water can be drawn up to the surface. There are risks, however. Water might drain from someplace else, creating even more desert.

Groundwater moves along underground layers called *aquifers*. Aquifers consist of earth materials or *pervious* (water-absorbing) rocks. There may be several layers separated by *impervious*, or hard, rock. Although it may move slowly, this way water can travel hundreds of miles. It may even have fallen as rain on distant mountains. When a well is drilled, the pressure of water in the aquifer can push the water up into the well. This is called an *artesian well*. If the pressure is so strong that water flows out above the ground, it is called a *flowing artesian well*.

Should there be a break in the rock above an aquifer, water may rise as a spring. The dry soil of the desert is often quite fertile, containing all the minerals needed for plants to grow. The addition of water may be enough to create an oasis. Some oases can only sustain a few families, but others are so large that cities have grown around them. River valleys provide the largest oases.

↓ A lush oasis in the Sahara Desert, in Algeria. There is enough water to grow date palms, and other crops, and to support a large number of people.

← An oasis in the Sahara, in Tunisia.

Many devices have been invented over the years to raise groundwater and distribute it over the land. Delivering water to the soil is called *irrigation*.

In developed countries, modern pumping methods are used to bring groundwater to the surface. But much older devices are still used in some parts of the world to raise water from wells or rivers. Some, like the *Persian wheel*, are operated by donkeys or oxen. The *Archimedean screw* is another ancient mechanical method of lifting water that is still in use today. In ancient China, people used to drill wells with hand tools.

Whether raised from underground or collected from the surface, water still needs to be distributed. The earliest forms of irrigation were canals or drainage ditches to take water to the crops. Nowadays, sprinklers are used. Another method is *drip irrigation*. Water is delivered to the plants through small holes or valves in plastic piping. It is fed only to the plants and not to the ground between them. Computers are now sometimes used to ensure that each plant receives the exact amount of water it needs. In the desert, not a drop can be wasted.

↑ *Persian wheel:* Waterwheels like this have been used for centuries.

→ Irrigation near the River Nile in Egypt. Water is being pumped directly from the river to the fields. Without irrigation, this land would be a desert.

← *Archimedean screw:* As the handle is turned, water is carried up the spiral inside the tube.

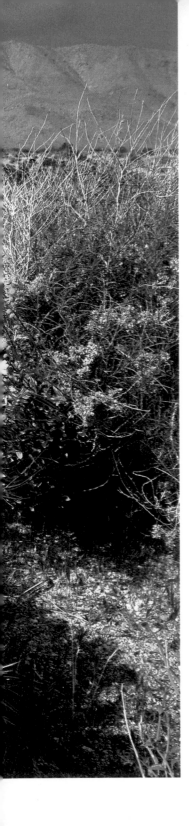

Desert plants have to make the most of the small amounts of water generally available, or of the occasional sudden downpour. To survive, they must be able to withstand extreme temperatures and long periods without rain.

One of nature's greatest spectacles is a desert in full bloom after heavy rains. Seeds lie buried, often for many years, awaiting the next rain. When it falls, the flowers blossom and die within weeks, dropping new seeds so that the cycle can be repeated when the rains return.

Like many other desert plants, the giant saguaro cactus soaks up amazing amounts of water from rare showers. Its roots are spread wide and are close to the surface in order to collect as much water as possible. It stores the water in its spongy stem. Its outer skin is ribbed so that the stem can expand or contract, according to how much water it contains. Many cacti have spikes to protect them from being eaten by animals.

Some desert plants store water in thick waxy stems or leaves. Others have to send roots deep down to search for water underground.

→ The gila woodpecker pecks a hole in a saguaro cactus to live in. The cactus provides the bird with food, water, and a home.

← The Mojave Desert in full bloom after heavy rains.

Animals of the Desert

Animals living in hot, dry deserts have to find ways of keeping cool. Cold-blooded reptiles, such as snakes and lizards, take on the temperature of their surroundings. Snakes are comfortable at very high temperatures, but even they have to find shade when the sun is at its hottest. Most lizards can't stand more than half an hour of sun at a time, so they divide their time between sunbathing and cooling off in the shade.

Many animals shelter from the sun in burrows during the day, coming out only in the cool of the night to search for food. Desert rodents such as gerbils, jerboas, and the long-legged American kangaroo rat, which hops like a tiny kangaroo, all dig burrows. Some hardly ever drink, but get water from foods such as seeds.

Spiders and their relatives, the scorpions, shelter in cracks in rocks, or simply hide beneath stones or sand. So do most insects, though some ants build nests consisting of a maze of tunnels deep underground.

The large ears of desert foxes, Australian bandicoots, and American jack rabbits enable them to detect danger a long way off. But their ears are not just for hearing. They have a network of veins close to the skin so the breeze can cool the animal's blood. Kangaroos have a similar network on their forearms, which they lick to keep their blood cool.

→ The scorpion is related to the spider. Its long body curls upward and its poisonous sting can kill a man.

↑ The desert fox, or fennec, is the world's smallest fox. It lives in the Arabian and Sahara deserts. It spends the day in a burrow, and comes out at night to hunt lizards, birds, and insects.

→ The sun spider is the world's fastest spider. It can run at over 25 miles per hour, faster than the lizards it feeds on.

← The elf owl lives in the deserts of America and Mexico. Only 6 inches long, it is the smallest owl in the world. It nests in a hole in a giant cactus abandoned by a gila woodpecker.

↑ Rattlesnakes live in American deserts. There are 28 kinds, including the small sidewinder snake. All of them have a rattle at the tip of the tail, made of loose rings of dry, horny skin. When the snake is frightened or angry, it shakes its tail and the rattling noise warns other animals to keep away.

The desert fox shelters in a burrow during the day. But bigger animals cannot hide from the sun, so they need other ways to keep cool. Thick hair or fur keeps the sun off their skin, and their large body area takes longer to warm up. Panting and sweating both have a cooling effect. But the body loses water when it sweats, so some of the larger animals only sweat when they are very hot. To get water, grazing animals such as antelopes and gazelles feed at night, since there is often dew on the ground then.

Birds are well-suited to desert life. Feathers screen their skin from the sun, and fluttering the throat helps them keep cool. Some get all the water they need from eating seeds or insects. Others fly long distances to oases or water holes.

One bird is able to carry water. The male sand grouse has spongy feathers on his belly. When he finds a pool, he gives them a good soaking. Then he flies back to his nest, which may be many miles away, so his chicks can suck the water from them.

Vultures are a common sight in most deserts. They do not kill for themselves. Instead, they circle for hours waiting for an animal to die or leave a meal unfinished.

← The roadrunner is a ground bird found in American deserts. It can sprint fast enough to catch mice, snakes, and lizards.

25

Many animals living in deserts have developed special tricks in order to survive. Some lizards, when they want to travel, "swim" through the sand to avoid the sun's heat. Desert rats and mice lick dew from pebbles. And the Kalahari ground squirrel uses its tail as an umbrella, curving it over its head, with the hairs fluffed out, to shield its body from the sun.

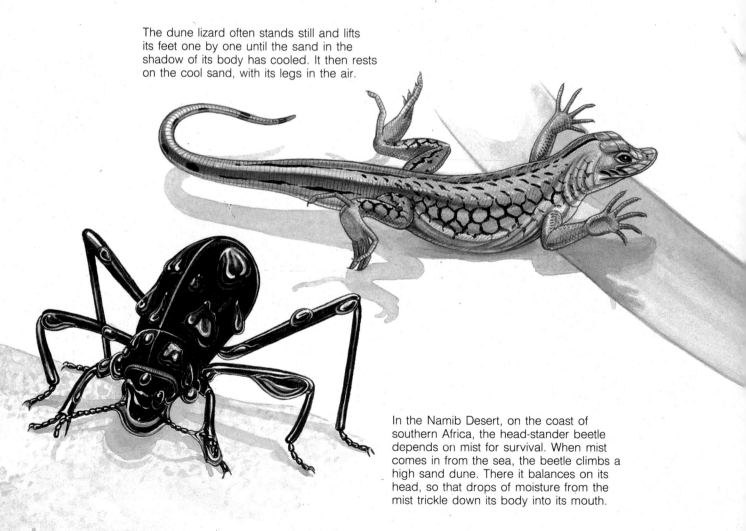

The dune lizard often stands still and lifts its feet one by one until the sand in the shadow of its body has cooled. It then rests on the cool sand, with its legs in the air.

In the Namib Desert, on the coast of southern Africa, the head-stander beetle depends on mist for survival. When mist comes in from the sea, the beetle climbs a high sand dune. There it balances on its head, so that drops of moisture from the mist trickle down its body into its mouth.

The sidewinder snake moves sideways across the sand, as can be seen from its tracks. As it moves, only parts of its body are in contact with the hot sand.

The American kangaroo rat has small front legs, a long hairy tail, and very long hind legs. It hops about like a tiny kangaroo. It hardly ever drinks, but gets water from seeds and juicy plants.

Spadefoot toads dig under the sand and produce a slimy coating of jelly to keep themselves moist, then sleep while they wait for rain. When it rains, perhaps months later, they wake up, mate, and lay their eggs. The new tadpoles grow up very quickly, in time to bury themselves before the water dries up.

27

↑ Visitors at the Pushkar camel fair enjoy the shade of a tree as they wait for the camel parades and races to start.

→ Camel drivers in action at Pushkar.

Camels and Camel Fairs

For thousands of years, camels have carried tents and baggage for travelers, bandits, and armies. Traders still cross the Sahara on camels in groups known as caravans, stopping at oases for food and water. In the 1850s, the U.S. Army tried using the camel in American deserts — unsuccessfully, since camel-handling was an unfamiliar skill.

Camels are deservedly called "ships of the desert." The one-humped Arabian camel, or dromedary, can plod along at 10 miles an hour for hours and carries loads of 500 pounds or more. Smaller dromedaries are bred for riding and racing. The Bactrian camel of central Asia has two humps. Its shaggy hair helps it survive in its cold, dry desert home.

Although automobiles are now widely used, camels are still important in desert life. As well as milk, butter, cheese, and meat, they supply leather and soft, fine wool for clothing, footwear, and tents.

In Africa and Asia, huge fairs are held where people buy, sell, and trade camels. Judgment and caution are needed in buying a camel. Just as a farmer is careful about choosing a tractor, so desert dwellers are careful to pick out the right camels for their needs.

Every November, a camel fair is held in Pushkar, on the edge of the Thar Desert in India. Some 25,000 camels, together with owners, families, and visitors, pack into the town. With its sideshows, brass bands, parades, and camel races, it is said to be the world's biggest and noisiest livestock show.

Fact File

Largest Deserts
The five largest deserts in the world are:

Sahara 3,250,000 square miles
Australian 600,000 square miles
Arabian 500,000 square miles
Gobi 400,000 square miles
Kalahari 200,000 square miles

Nearly one eighth of the Earth's land surface is covered by desert. The Sahara is more than 30 times larger than New York State.

Creeping Deserts
Each year, the world's deserts take over about 27,000 square miles of farmland. The Sahara, for example, is spreading steadily southward and is rapidly engulfing Mauritania, a country four times the size of Colorado.

Riches Under the Deserts
In most of the world's deserts few people can even make a living. Yet beneath some deserts lie great riches, such as gold, silver, copper, diamonds, oil, and natural gas.

The richest oilfields in the world have been found under the deserts of Saudi Arabia and other parts of the Middle East.

↓ A desert oil rig

Highest Temperature Ever
The highest temperature ever recorded was 136.4°F at Al Aziziyah, on the edge of the Sahara Desert in Libya in 1922.

Cooler Down Below
Readings taken in California's Mojave Desert showed that, while the temperature was 150°F at the surface, it was a cool 60°F in a burrow only 18 inches below ground. No wonder so many desert animals hide in burrows during the day!

The Driest Place on Earth
The Atacama Desert in Chile and Peru has an average annual rainfall of less than ½ inch. In many years there is no rain at all. Until 1971, some parts of the Atacama had had no rain since the 16th century.

Mushroom Rocks
In some rocky deserts, you will find rocks shaped like mushrooms. These are formed by the wind blowing grains of sand along just above the

↓ Mushroom rock

↑ Harvesting dates

ground. The sand wears away the base of the rocks over thousands or millions of years, until they look like huge mushrooms with slender stalks.

Dust Storms
Strong winds blowing across deserts often raise great clouds of sand, dust and grit. These clouds are sometimes carried enormous distances and can be large enough to blot out the sun.

When the wind is blowing toward Europe, people there sometimes find their cars or houses covered with fine red dust blown all the way from the Sahara.

Dust Devils
Sometimes a light wind picks up a small spiralling column of dust that dances along the ground. This is called a "dust devil."

The Tree of Life
The tree you most often see growing in the oases of the Middle East and northern Africa is the date palm. The leaves are woven into articles such as mats and baskets. The bark fiber makes strong rope, and both the leaves and trunk are used as building materials. The dates themselves may be eaten fresh or dried and are easy to preserve. The date palm has so many uses that in Muslim writings it is called "the Tree of Life."

The History of the Sahara
Rock paintings, carvings, tools, and other objects found in the Sahara prove that it was once a land of green fields and trees. In fact, the Sahara only started to turn into a desert about 6,000 years ago, due to a change in climate.

Millions of years ago, the land occupied by the Sahara was where the South Pole is now. This is because each year the Earth's continents move a few inches. Over millions of years, this transforms the map of the world.

Index

Picture Credits
N.S. Barrett: page 30 (right)
BP: 30 (left)
GeoScience Features: B. Booth 12
Hutchison Library: Sarah Errington 1
Pat Morris: 22-23
Remote Source: C.S. Caldicott 8-9, 28, 28-29
Royal Geographical Society: 4-5
Survival Anglia: Mark Anderson 6-7
Zefa (UK) Ltd: 11, 14-15, 15, 16, 17, 18, 19, 20-21, 24-25, 31